# Keto Ice Creams

*Amazingly Delicious Ice Creams and Frozen Treats for Your Low-Carb High Fat Life*

**Faith Smith**

# Introduction

With summer here with us, nothing beats the heat than having a cold treat in the afternoon as you enjoy the warm weather. The challenge for many however, especially those on a diet and not wanting to over-indulge is finding a frozen treat that is not only sweet but also healthy.

This is why I created this book. I love ice creams and everything frozen. However, when I adopted the ketogenic diet, I had to look for healthier and keto-friendly ice creams and frozen treats to enjoy.

This book is a compilation of some of the my favorite frozen treats and ice creams that are not only delicious but also healthy, keto-friendly and relatively easy to make.

I hope you enjoy the recipes.

against the publisher for any reparation, damages, or monetary loss due to the information herein, either directly or indirectly.

Respective authors own all copyrights not held by the publisher.

The information herein is offered for informational purposes solely, and is universal as so. The presentation of the information is without contract or any type of guarantee assurance.

The trademarks that are used are without any consent, and the publication of the trademark is without permission or backing by the trademark owner. All trademarks and brands within this book are for clarifying purposes only and are the owned by the owners themselves, not affiliated with this document.

# Table of Contents

Introduction....................................................2

Fruity Ice Creams.............................................9

   Light Berry Frozen Yogurt...........................9

   Frozen Fruit Ice Cream................................11

   Avocado Sorbet .........................................13

   Blueberry Ice Cream....................................15

   Lemon Curd Ice Cream ..............................17

   Strawberry Ice Cream.................................19

   Strawberry Nutella Ice Cream......................21

   Avocado Ice Cream ....................................23

   Lemon Ice Cream ......................................24

Chocolate and Vanilla Ice Creams.....................27

   Chocolate Chip Ice Cream ..........................27

   Chocolate Almond Ice Cream ......................29

   Dairy-Free Chocolate Ice Cream..................31

   Avocado Chocolate Chip Ice-Cream............33

Chocolate Toffee Ice Cream..................................36

Keto Chocolate Ice Cream ...............................39

Mint Chocolate Chip Ice Cream.............................41

Tasty Chocolate Ice Cream ...............................43

Black Forest Ice Cream ...............................46

Easy No-Churn Vanilla Ice Cream............................48

Keto Vanilla Ice Cream...............................50

Vanilla Flavored Ice Cream ...............................52

Ultimate Keto Fat Bomb Ice Cream..........................54

Egg Fast Vanilla Frozen Custard.............................57

Popsicles and Ice Cream Bars.................................59

Strawberry Cheesecake Popsicles ............................59

Yogurt Pops...............................61

Peanut Butter Popsicles ...............................64

Almond Milk Popsicles ...............................67

Fudge Popsicles...............................68

Sugar-Free Fudge Pops ...............................69

Yogurt Pops .................................................................. 72

Coconut Milk Popsicles.................................................. 75

Raspberry Ice Cream Bars.............................................. 77

Avocado Ice Cream Bars................................................ 79

Toasted Almond Ice Cream Bars ................................... 81

Homemade Snickers Ice Cream Bars ............................. 83

Yogurt Berry Ice Blocks................................................. 87

Peanut Butter Ice Cream Bars ........................................ 89

Low-Carb Ice Cream Bars.............................................. 91

Keto Ice Cream Bars ..................................................... 93

Mocha Ice Cream Bars ................................................... 95

Iced Coffee and Tea Frozen Treats................................. 98

Coffee Panna Cotta with Raspberry ............................... 98

Mocha Ice Cream ......................................................... 100

Coffee Ice Cream.......................................................... 102

Keto Coffee Ice Cream................................................. 105

Dairy-Free Coffee Ice Cream ....................................... 107

Green Tea Ice Cream .................................................... 109

Conclusion ................................................................. 111

About The Author ....................................................... 112

My Other Books .......................................................... 113

# Fruity Ice Creams

## Light Berry Frozen Yogurt

*Prep Time 15 minutes*

*Total Time 15 minutes*

*Serves 6*

*Ingredients*

4 droppers full vanilla liquid stevia

1 cup ice

1/2 cup milk 1%

1 cup plain yogurt

2 cups frozen berries

*Optional toppings:*

Chopped nuts

Homemade Magic Shell,

Whipped Cream chocolate chunks or chips

*Directions*

1. Add everything into a high speed blender or use 2 cups of thawed frozen berries to blend in a food processor or regular blender.

2. As soon as it is well-blended, add the mixture into the ice cream maker and churn accordingly.

3. Alternatively, pour the mixture into an airtight container and keep it frozen for approximately 2 to 3 hours, while covered.

*Calories 76, Carbs 10g, Protein 3g, Fat 3g*

# Frozen Fruit Ice Cream

*Prep Time: 5 minutes*

*Total Time: 5 minutes*

*Serves: 2*

*Ingredients*

1/8 teaspoon monk fruit powder or stevia powder

1/2 cup heavy cream or coconut cream

1 cup frozen berries

*Directions*

1. Add 1 cup of frozen fruit into the food processor and blend for a couple of seconds until everything is fully broken down into pieces.

2. Add in stevia powder and heavy cream and process until you get smooth and creamy ice cream, or for about 20 to 30 seconds.

3. In case your food processor or blender is stuck, move the ice cream around using a spoon and then continue to blend.

4. Serve and enjoy!

*Keto Ice Creams*

*Calories: 242, Carbs: 9.76g, Protein: 2.19g, Fat: 22.37g*

# Avocado Sorbet

*Prep time 15 minutes*

*Total time 15 minutes*

*Serves 5*

*Ingredients*

½ teaspoon Celtic sea salt

1 teaspoon mango extract

2 tablespoons lime juice

¾ cup Swerve

2 ripe avocados

2 cups almond milk, unsweetened

*Directions*

1. Put all the ingredients in a blender or food processor and blend until smooth.

2. Then move the contents to the cold container of your ice cream maker and churn as per the directions.

3. Once done, move the cooled container to the freezer and keep it frozen.

4. In case you feel that the ice cream isn't as sweet, adjust the sweetener and then return to the freezer.

*Calories 146, Carbs 8.2g, Protein 2g, Fat 13.2g*

# Blueberry Ice Cream

*Prep Time 20 minutes*

*Cook Time 5 minutes*

*Total Time 25 minutes*

*Serves 8*

*Ingredients*

1/2 teaspoon xanthan gum, optional

1/3 cup almond milk or coconut milk, unsweetened

1 13.5 can coconut cream

1 cup blueberries

2/3 cup LC Foods white sweetener – inulin

1 lime

*Directions*

1. In a medium sized sauce pan, grate the lime well and squeeze the lemon juice into the pan.

2. In a mixing bowl, put the cream layer from the coconut cream can and whip until you obtain stiff peaks.

3. Now pour some of the liquid from the coconut cream into the saucepan along with lime.

4. Then stir in the blueberries, the white sweetener and almond milk or coconut milk.

5. Heat the mixture to boiling and cook the mixture on gentle boil while stirring now and again for approximately 4 minutes.

6. Remove the contents from heat and now whisk in xanthan gum if you like. Let it cool for some time and the whisk in the coconut cream.

7. Put the contents in an ice bath or the fridge until fully chilled.

8. Then process the mixture in the ice cream machine as per the manufacturer's instructions.

9. You can also chill out in the container overnight so as it help separate cream from the liquid.

*Calories 185, Carbs 14.3g, Protein 1.2g, Fat 14g*

# Lemon Curd Ice Cream

*Prep Time: 35 minutes*

*Cook Time: 10 minutes*

*Chill Time 4 hours*

*Total Time: 4 hours 45 minutes*

*Servings: 10*

*Ingredients*

1/3 cup powdered Swerve Sweetener

1 1/2 cup heavy whipping cream

2 tablespoons vodka, optional

*Directions*

1.Whisk together powdered sweetener, whipping cream and the lemon curd in a large bowl until fully mixed. Add in some vodka if you like.

2. Move the mixture into your ice cream maker and churn as per the manufacturer's recommendations.

3.Then move the mixture into an airtight container and keep it frozen for 2 to 3 hours, to firm up.

4.If you find the leftovers becoming too hard, let the ice cream sit for 15 to 20 minutes on room temperature.

*Calories 308, Carbs 2.47g, Protein 4.56g, Fat 29.55g*

# Strawberry Ice Cream

*Prep Time: 15 minutes*

*Chill Time 1-2 hours*

*Total Time: 1 hour 15 minutes*

*Serves 16*

*Ingredients*

1/2-3/4 cup equivalent sweetener

16 oz frozen strawberries

2 cans (13.5 oz) coconut milk

1/2 cup chopped fresh strawberries, optional

*Directions*

1. Add everything to a high as speed blender apart from the strawberries and process until smooth.

2. Put the mixture into the ice cream machine and now churn according to its makers instructions.

3. Then add in the strawberries a few seconds before you're done with mixing the ice cream.

4. Serve the ice cream instantly or instead keep it frozen until hard, or for approximately 1 to 2 hours.

*Calories 42, Carb 10.6g, Protein 0.5g, Fat 0.2g*

# Strawberry Nutella Ice Cream

*Prep Time: 10 minutes*

*Cook Time: 6 hours*

*Total Time: 6 hours*

*Serves:8 (1 large loaf pan)*

*Ingredients*

1 lb. strawberries cut into small pieces

2 cups cold heavy cream

1/2 cup Nutella

1 teaspoon pure vanilla extract

1 can, 14 ounces condensed milk, sweetened

*Directions*

1. Whisk together vanilla and condensed milk in a medium sized bowl.

2. Then beat the heavy cream in a large bowl with an electric mixer for 3 minutes on high heat, or until stiff peaks form.

3. Slowly fold the whipped cream into the vanilla and milk mixture, and blend the contents using a spatula.

4. Add in the chopped strawberries and nutella. Carefully mix together and then pour the mixture into a loaf pan.

5. Keep the ice cream frozen for around  hours or until firm.

*Calories 135, Carb 6.5g, Protein 1.2g, Fat 11.9g*

# Avocado Ice Cream

*Prep Time: 15 minutes*

*Chill Time 1-2 hours*

*Total Time: 1 hour 15 minutes*

*Ingredients*

10g or 1/4 cup fresh mint leaves, loosely packed

10g or 1/4 cup fresh basil leaves, loosely packed

25g or juice from 1/2 lemon

25g or 2 generous tablespoons MCT oil

250g or 8.5 oz. can unsweetened full fat coconut milk

150g or 2 small ripe avocados

A sweetener of your choice, optional

Pinch of salt

*Directions*

1. Begin by removing any skin and pits from your avocados and then blend the fruit along with the rest of the ingredients

until smooth. Scrap the sides of the blender a couple of times until done.

2. Pour the mixture into an ice cream machine and run until its frozen. Serve the ice cream immediately.

3. In case you don't have an ice cream maker or if intending to keep the ice cream frozen in smaller amounts, you can pour the mixture into ice cube trays or popsicle mods and keep it frozen.

*Calories 100, Carb 12g, Protein 7g, Fat 92g*

## Lemon Ice Cream

*Prep Time: 30 minutes*

*Total Time: 30 minutes*

*Serves: 8*

*Ingredients*

½ teaspoon salt *to keep ice cream soft

1 lime, zested

1 teaspoon fresh cilantro, chopped

Drop of stevia glycerite, optional

1 teaspoon ginger, freshly grated

1 stalk lemongrass

½ teaspoon fish sauce

4 egg yolks

4 whole eggs

½ cup coconut milk or homemade bone broth

4 tablespoons MCT oil

¾ cup + 2 tablespoons organic butter or coconut oil

*Directions*

1. Add cilantro, teaspoon of lime zest, 1 lime, ginger, lemon grass, coconut milk, eggs, MCT oil, coconut oil and salt to a blender.

2. Blend well until smooth and creamy and then move the mixture into a cream machine and churn well.

3. Remove from the machine and store it frozen in airtight containers until ready to serve.

*Calories 290, Carb 0.9g, Protein 4.7g,  Fat 30g*

# Chocolate and Vanilla Ice Creams

## Chocolate Chip Ice Cream

*Prep Time: 15 minutes*

*Total Time: 15 minutes*

*Serves 16*

*Ingredients*

3/4 cup chopped almonds

4 cups coconut milk

1/2 - 3/4 cup xylitol

3/4 cup chocolate chips

1/4 teaspoon salt

1 teaspoon vanilla

1 tablespoon gelatin or arrowroot

1-3 tablespoons MCT oil

3/4 cup cocoa

*Directions*

1.Add in coconut milk, vanilla, gelatin, MCT oil, cocoa powder and the xylitol sweetener in a food processor or blender.

2. In case you are using gelatin, add it to coconut milk and allow it to sit for a couple of minutes and then add to the rest of the ingredients. Combine well.

3. Move the mixture into the ice cream machine and churn as per the manufacturer's directions.

4. As soon as the ice cream mixture begins to thicken, add in chocolate chips and the almonds.

*Calories 106, Carb 11.4g, Protein 4.4g, Fat 7.2g*

# Chocolate Almond Ice Cream

*Prep Time: 15 minutes*

*Chill Time 2 hours*

*Total Time: 2 hours 15 minutes*

*Ingredients*

3 tablespoons erythritol

4 tablespoons of sweetener–

1/4 cup of lite coconut milk or liquid egg whites

2 tablespoons cocoa powder

1/4 teaspoon pure vanilla extract

1/2 teaspoon pure almond extract

1 cup of ricotta or cottage cheese

Optional:

1/4 teaspoon pure stevia extract

1 tablespoon glycerin

*Directions*

1. Mix together all the ingredients into a magic bullet or a blender. Mix until smooth and lump-free while you scrap down the processor a number of times.

2. Keep the mixture frozen as per the instructions of the ice cream maker.

3. Store the ice cream frozen in a tupperware container and serve it chilled or within 2 hours unless if you want it to turn into an icy rock.

4. You can add a tablespoon of vodka to prevent hardening, or pop the icy rock ice cream to your microwave for a couple of seconds.

*Calories 67, Carb 9g, Protein 2.4g, Fat 2.7g*

# Dairy-Free Chocolate Ice Cream

*Prep Time 5 minutes*

*Total Time 5 minutes*

*Servings 2*

*Ingredients*

Cacao nibs, optional

1 pinch salt

1 teaspoon chocolate stevia

2 tablespoons cocoa powder, unsweetened

1 can coconut milk

*Directions*

1. Combine together all the ingredients in your blender.

2. Then slowly pour the contents into your ice cream maker and churn as per its manufacturer's directions.

3. Serve the ice cream immediately!

*Calories 318, Carbs 9.1g, Protein 3g, Fat 28.6g*

# Avocado Chocolate Chip Ice-Cream

*Prep Time: 15 minutes*

*Cook Time: 30 minutes*

*Chill Time 1 hour*

*Total Time: 1 hours 45 minutes*

*Serves 8*

*Ingredients*

1 package dark chocolate chips, or chopped 85% dark chocolate bar

1/4 cup 1 tablespoon mint extract or fresh mint

1 tablespoon seeds from 1 vanilla bean or sugar-free vanilla extract

15-20 drops Stevia extract

1/2 cup Erythritol or Swerve, powdered

2 cups (1 can) heavy whipping cream or coconut milk

2 large ripe avocados

*Directions*

1. Cut the well ripe avocado in half, and then scoop the pulp into a medium bowl.

2. Then add in powdered Erythritol, mint, coconut milk and stevia. You should add in the whole can of coconut along with the water.

3. Now add in the spearmint or mint extract and the vanilla.

4. Process the ingredients until well blended. Add the contents to your ice cream machine and process for approximately 30 to 60 minutes or as per the manufacturer's directions.

5. In the meantime, begin chopping the dark chocolate into smaller pieces or instead try using some chocolate chips.

6. As soon as the ice cream making is done, add in the chopped chocolate and blend it well with a spatula.

7. Keep the ice cream frozen until soft, or for 30 to 60 minutes. You can serve instantly or instead keep it frozen in the freezer for not more than 3 months.

8. To serve the frozen ice cream, just microwave for approximately 10 to 20 seconds or instead let it come to room temperature for at least 20 minutes.

*Calories 264, Carbs 5.6g, Protein 3.6g, Fat 25.2g*

# Chocolate Toffee Ice Cream

*Prep time 10 min*

*Total time 8 hours 20 min*

*Servings 8*

*Ingredients*

1/4 cup chopped toffee, sugar free

1/4 cup fried crisp and chopped bacon

1.5 oz. of 90% dark chocolate

Pinch of salt

1 1/2 cups + 2 tablespoons heavy whipping cream, divided

1 cup unsweetened vanilla almond milk

1/2 teaspoon xanthan gum

1 cup premium cocoa powder

3 large eggs

1 cup granulated sugar substitute

8 oz. Hickory Bacon

## Directions

1. Mix together cocoa butter, eggs, granulated sugar substitute, almond milk and xanthan gum in a blender and puree until smooth,

2. Move the mixture to a heat safe dish and microwave on high heat for a minute. Stir the contents for about 1/2 a minute and repeat until you obtain a thick mixture.

3. In case you find lumps, stir thoroughly or instead run through a strainer to remove the lumps.

4. Now whisk in 1.5 cups of heavy cream and a pinch of salt. Cover the contents well and keep it refrigerated for more than 8 hours.

5. Start mixing the reserved 2 tablespoons of heavy cream with the chocolate in a heat safe bowl and then microwave on high heat settings for approximately 30 seconds.

6. Once melted, stir and then and in some bacon, stir again and then cover a baking sheet with a wax paper.

7. Spread the heavy cream and chocolate mixture on the prepared baking sheet and keep it refrigerated for approximately 10 minutes, or until hard. Then chop the hardened mixture and set aside.

8. As soon as the egg and almond milk mixture is completely chilled, run it into your ice cream maker and then churn as per its maker's directions.

9. In the late 1 to 2 minutes of churning, add in the toffee and chocolate bacon chops.

*10.* Serve the ice cream immediately or keep it frozen until hardened. To serve, just defrost it for around 15 minutes at room temperature and then eat!

*Calories 191; Carbs 9.7g; Protein 11.7g, Fat 9.8g*

# Keto Chocolate Ice Cream

*Prep Time: 35 minutes*

*Total Time: 35 minutes*

*Serves 1*

*Ingredients:*

2 teaspoons vanilla powder

1/4 – 1/3 cup cocoa powder

1/4 cup filtered water or ice

3.5 tablespoons granulated sweetener of choice

3 tablespoons + 2 teaspoons coconut oil, melted

6 tablespoons + 1 scant teaspoon XCT oil

3.5 tablespoons cacao butter, melted

7 tablespoons ghee or grass-fed butter, melted

1 teaspoon apple cider vinegar or lemon juice

4 or 5 pasture-raised egg yolks

4 pasture-raised eggs

1 or 2 teaspoons cinnamon, optional

*Directions*

1. Add everything into a high speed blender beginning with the 30 grams of preferred sweetener. Process for approximately 1 to 2 minutes.

2. Taste and adjust the flavor if required, and then move the mixture into an ice cream machine.

3. Churn the ice cream for approximately 15 to 20 minutes and then enjoy.

*Calories 177, Carb 3.7g, Protein 2.7g, Fat 14g*

# Mint Chocolate Chip Ice Cream

*Prep Time: 15 minutes*

*Chill Time: 2 hours*

*Serves: 2 scoops*

*Ingredients*

30-45g chopped cacao nibs, or chocolate chips

2-4 tablespoons powdered xylitol

1 pinch flakey sea salt or salt of choice

1/2 teaspoon freshly squeezed lemon juice

1/2-3/4 teaspoon peppermint extract

1/2 teaspoon vanilla extract

50g avocado

110g heavy cream or full-fat coconut milk

*Directions*

1. First pop the coconut milk in quick water bath so as to remove any solids. Bring the milk back to room temperature and add it to an immersion blender.

2. Now add in lemon juice, peppermint extract, vanilla extract, salt and the powdered xylitol to the coconut milk.

3. Blend the contents until you obtain smooth and creamy mixture.

4. Move the mixture to seal-able container and keep frozen for approximately 2x hours or until set.

5. In case you are freezing it overnight, just ensure you bring it to room temperature before serving.

*Calories 151, Carbs 3.5g, Protein 1.5g, Fat 15g*

# Tasty Chocolate Ice Cream

*Prep Time 15 minutes*

*Cook Time 20 minutes*

*Chilling time 6 hours*

*Total Time 35 minutes*

*Servings: 8*

*Ingredients*

1/4 to 1/2 teaspoon liquid stevia extract

1/2 teaspoon vanilla extract

3 ounces chocolate chopped, unsweetened

4 large egg yolks

1/2 cup Swerve Sweetener

1/2 cup cocoa powder

1 1/2 cups unsweetened almond or coconut milk, divided

2 cups heavy cream

2 tablespoons vodka, optional

1/4 teaspoon xanthan gum, optional

*Directions*

1. Put a bowl over an ice bath for a few minutes.

2. Then mix together a cup of cashew milk, cream, xanthan gum and cocoa powder in a medium sauce pan.

3. Whisk the mixture until fully blended and then stir until it gets to 170 degrees F on an instant thermometer.

4. Then in a medium bowl, whisk some egg yolks and then add in a cup of the hot cashew milk and cream mixture. Whisk over and over again to blend the yolks with the mixture.

5. Add the blended egg yolks into the saucepan, and continue to whisk until the mixture is thick enough to coat a spoon and indicates 175 degrees F on a thermometer.

6. Take out the ice cream mixture from heat and add in the chocolate. Allow the mixture sit for about 5 minutes and then whisk until incorporated.

7. Now pour the mixture into the prepared bowl put over the ice bath for approximately 10 minutes. Wrap it well in plastic and keep it chilled for more than 3 hours.

8. Whisk in vanilla extract, stevia mixture, 1/2 cup of cashew milk and the vodka if you like to help thin the ice cream. Cover the surface with the xanthan gum and whisk fully to blend.

9. Now move the mixture into your ice cream maker and churn as per its maker's recommendations.

10. Then serve instantly or instead store in an airtight container and keep frozen for 1 to 2 hours or until its firm.

*Calories 303, Carbs 9.1g, Protein 4.4g, Fat 27.2g*

# **Black Forest Ice Cream**

*Prep Time: 10 minutes*

*Total Time: 10 minutes*

*Serves 6*

*Ingredients*

1/3 cup grated dark chocolate

1/4 cup cocoa powder, unsweetened

1/2 cup powdered erythritol or Confectioner's Style Swerve

1 tablespoon cherry flavoring

400 ml organic coconut milk

*Directions*

1. In a large bowl, combine the cherry flavoring, coconut milk and the sweetener.

2. Add the rest of the ingredients and stir until incorporated.

3. Move the contents into your ice cream maker and churn accordingly.

4. Serve the ice cream with some grated chocolate and whipped cream. You should keep any leftovers frozen.

*Calories 150, Carbs 2g, Protein 3.9g, Fat 13.8g*

# Easy No-Churn Vanilla Ice Cream

*Prep Time: 5 minutes*

*Total Time: 6 hours 10 minutes*

*Serves 4*

*Ingredients*

1 1/2 teaspoons pure vanilla extract, divided

4 tablespoons monk fruit sweetener, divided

2 scoops Perfect Keto Vanilla Collagen, divided

2 cups heavy whipping cream, divided

*Directions*

1. Begin by adding ¾ teaspoon of vanilla extract, a scoop of collagen powder, 2 tablespoons of sweetener and a cup of heavy cream into 2 wide-mouth mason jars.

2. Shake the mixture well for approximately 5 minutes.

3. Move the mason jars to the freezer and keep frozen for approximately 4 to 6 hours or until solid.

4. Keep shaking the cream around every 2 hours. Serve the ice cream while chilled.

*Calories: 440, Carbs: 4.40g, Protein: 7.45g, Fat: 46.05g*

## Keto Vanilla Ice Cream

*Prep Time: 15 minutes*

*Total Time: 15 minutes*

*Serves: 5-6*

*Ingredients*

100 grams water or ice

5.5 tablespoons xylitol or erythritol

3 tablespoons + 2 teaspoons XCT oil

100 grams coconut oil

100 grams or 7 tablespoons grass-fed butter

1 gram vitamin C or 10 drops lime juice or apple cider vinegar

2 teaspoons vanilla powder

4 yolks

4 whole pastured eggs

1/4 to 1/2 cup of low-toxin cocoa powder, optional

*Directions*

1. Add all the ingredients into the blender apart from the ice or water.

2. Blend fully until the butter is fully incorporated into the creamy mixture.

3. Then add in ice or water and blend well. You can add extra amount of water in case you want to get a harder icier cream, or add yogurt to get an ice cream consistency.

4. Transfer the mixture to your ice cream machine and churn until ready to serve.

*Calories: 539, Carbs: 3.1g, Protein: 8.64g, Fat: 55.8g*

## **Vanilla Flavored Ice Cream**

*Prep Time: 10 minutes*

*Total Time: 10 minutes*

*Serves 4-5*

*Ingredients*

1 1/2 teaspoon vanilla bean paste or pure vanilla extract

1/8 teaspoon salt

1/3 cup erythritol, xylitol, or other natural sweetener

2 cups canned coconut milk, full-fat

*Directions*

1. Stir together full-fat canned coconut milk with vanilla extract and salt.

2. In case you have an ice machine, churn the mixture based on the manufacturer's directions.

3. If not having an ice cream machine, simply freeze the coconut milk and vanilla extract mixture in ice tube trays.

4. In a Vitamix or other high speed blender, blend the frozen cubes for a few seconds or thaw them for some time before processing in a regular food processor.

4. Serve or chill for an hour or so to obtain a firmer texture. Eat it on the same day or chill any leftovers up to a month to avoid going bad.

*Calories 86, Carbs 7.4g, Protein 3.8g, Fat 4g*

## Ultimate Keto Fat Bomb Ice Cream

*Prep time: 60 minutes*

*Cooling time: 2 to 3 hours*

*Total time: 3 hours*

*Serves: 5*

*Ingredients*

8-10 ice cubes

2 teaspoons vanilla bean powder

¼ cup MCT oil

1/3 cup flavor variation

1/3 cup xylitol or 15-20 drops of alcohol-free stevia

1/3 cup melted coconut oil

1/3 cup melted cacao butter

4 yolks from pastured eggs

4 whole pastured eggs

*Directions*

1. Add all of the ingredients into the jug of a Vitamix or other high powered blended apart from the ice cubes.

2. Process on high speed until creamy, or for about 2 minutes or so.

3. Remove the top portion of the lid with the blender still running and aid in all the ice cubes one at a time.

4. Let the blender run for about 10 seconds between each of the ice cubes. If your blender has no hole on the lid, turn it off with each addition of the ice cube one piece at a time.

5. As soon as you have added all ice cubes, pour the mixture into the ice cream machine and churn on high speed for around 20 to 30 minutes.

6. Alternatively, move the mixture into a 9 by 5-loaf pan and keep in a freezer for approximately 30 minutes. Stir and repeat for another 2 to 3 hours until you get your preferred consistency.

7. Serve it immediately as a soft serve and enjoy!

8. Alternatively, you can scoop to a 9 by 5 inch pan and keep frozen for another 45 minutes. Store any leftovers covered in the freezer for less than 7 days.

*Keto Ice Creams*

*Calories 485, Carbs 7.48g, Protein 9.47g, Fat 48.76g*

# Egg Fast Vanilla Frozen Custard

*Prep Time 5 minutes*

*Cook Time 15 minutes*

*Total Time 20 minutes*

*Servings 4*

*Ingredients*

1/2 teaspoon vanilla extract

4 eggs

1/4 teaspoon of monk fruit liquid extract

1/4 teaspoon cream of tartar

1/2 teaspoon vanilla stevia drops

4 ounces unsalted butter

4 ounces cream cheese

*Directions*

1. Begin by separating the eggs.

2. Then over low heat, heat butter, cheese and egg yolks while whisking regularly until the mixture is thick.

3. Remove the contents from heat and then stir in vanilla and your preferred sweetener.

4. Then to the egg whites, add in cream of tartar and whip until you obtain a soft mixture.

5. Beat in the cheese and egg yolk mixture into the soft egg white mixture.

6. At this point, pour the mixture into a freezer container that has a lid. Keep it frozen for approximately 2 hour, while stirring the frozen edges in.

7. Return the ice cream to the freezer for 1 more hour. Then process it in your ice cream maker until it reaches the constituency you want.

*Calories 326, Carbs 1.5g, Protein 9.7g, Fat 31.6g*

# Popsicles and Ice Cream Bars

## Strawberry Cheesecake Popsicles

*Prep Time 15 minutes*

*Chill time 4 hours*

*Total Time 4 hours 15 minutes*

*Serves 12 Popsicles*

*Ingredients*

2 cups fresh strawberries chopped, divided

2 teaspoons lemon zest

1 tablespoons lemon juice

1/4 teaspoon monk fruit extract or stevia extract

1/3 cup powdered Swerve Sweetener

1 cup cream

8 oz. cream cheese softened

*Directions*

1. In a food processor, add in the cream cheese and blend until smooth.

2. Add lemon zest, lemon juice, powdered swerve, cream and the stevia extract. Process the mixture until well blended.

3. Add 1 and 1/2 cups of the strawberries to the mixture and blend until almost smooth, and then add the rest of the strawberries.

4. Pour the mixture into perspective wooden popsicle molds and then push the sticks approximately 2/3 way each.

5. Keep the ice cream frozen for a minimum of 4 hours.

6. Then unmold the Popsicles under hot water for about 20 to 30 minutes and then twist the stick gently so as to release.

*Calories 122, Carbs 3g, Protein 2g, Fat 12g*

# Yogurt Pops

*Prep Time: 35 minutes*

*Cook Time: 10 minutes*

*Chill Time 2 hours*

*Total Time: 2 hours 45 minutes*

*Yields 12 popsicles*

*Ingredients*

1/2 teaspoon vanilla

25 drops stevia extract

18 oz Greek yogurt

3.5 oz 85 % cacao chocolate, finely chopped

1/4 cup powdered erythritol

2 tablespoons cocoa powder

1/2 cup whipping cream

*Directions*

1. Mix together powdered erythritol, cocoa powder and whipped in a small saucepan over medium heat and whisk until smooth.

2. Heat it the mixture through but not to an extent of a simmer. Then add in the chocolate and let the mixture sit until melted, or for around 2 minutes.

3. Now whisk the mixture until smooth. Based on the chocolate, you may need to increase the heat a bit and then additional cream a tablespoon at each addition. Then whisk completely until smooth.

4. Then mix together stevia, vanilla extract and Greek yogurt in a medium bowl.

5. Stir until the chocolate is well incorporated into the mixture. Now pipe or spoon the well-blended mixture into popsicle molds, and then sticks.

6. Keep the popsicle sticks frozen for a minimum 2 hours or until solid.

7. You can also keep mixture refrigerated for 1-2 hours and then churn it as per your ice cream maker's instructions.

*Calories 87, Carbs 7.23g, Protein 5.54g, Fat 4.6g*

## **Peanut Butter Popsicles**

*Prep Time 20 minutes*

*Chill Time 4 hours*

*Total Time 4 hours 20 minutes*

*Servings 12 Popsicles*

*Ingredients*

1/2 ounce cocoa butter chopped

4 ounces  chopped dark chocolate, sugar-free

3/4 cup heavy cream

1/2 teaspoon vanilla extract

1/2 cup  Swerve Sweetener, powdered

1 cup creamy peanut butter

8 oz. cream cheese softened

*Directions*

1. Beat together peanut butter, vanilla extract, powdered Swerve Sweetener, heavy cream and cream cheese until well incorporated and smooth.

2. Spoon the mixture to approximately 12 and 15 popsicle molds and then tap the molds well on the counter to let any air bubbles escape.

3. Put the popsicles in the center of each wooden stick and keep frozen until frozen or until firm.

4. Then remove the molds by running them under hot water or instead put them in a bowl with hot water. Release and the twist the sticks to release.

5. Keep the popsicle sticks in the freezer until you're ready to dip them into the chopped dark chocolate.

6. Then get a waxed paper or parchment paper and line your baking sheet well before putting them in the freezer.

7. Set a ceramic bowl or metal bowl over the saucepan that has simmering water. Ensure that the bottom of the bowl does not touch the water.

8. Then add in cocoa butter and chopped chocolate and stir until the chocolate has melted. Remove the mixture from heat.

9. At this point, dip a popsicles into individual chocolates approximately halfway, and then allow any excess chocolate to drip back into the bowl.

10. Once the chocolate is firm, put the well done popsicle on the cookie sheet and move to the freezer and repeat the process with the rest of the popsicle sticks.

*Calories 280, Carbs 8.7g, Protein 5.6g, Fat 24.9g*

# Almond Milk Popsicles

*Prep Time: 10 minutes*

*Total Time: 10 minutes*

*Servings 10*

*Ingredients*

3/4 cup almond milk, unsweetened

1 teaspoon natural root beer flavor

1 teaspoon vanilla extract

1/4 cup granulated stevia/erythritol blend

3/4 cup organic and grass-fed heavy whipping cream

*Directions*

1. Add cream into a mixing bowl and then whip it with an electric mixer until you see stiff peaks.

2. Add in vanilla extract, the stevia or erythritol, and the beer flavoring. Now beat the mix until fully blended.

3. Add in milk and process until well mixed and you obtain a thin creamy mixture.

4. Then whip the contents until it becomes frothy and begins to slowly thicken.

5. At this point, pour the thick mixture into mold, and add the popsicle sticks. Once done, keep everything frozen for a few hours and then serve.

6. To serve, just run hot water over the outside of the molds to release the Popsicles.

*Calories: 70, Carbs: 2.7g, Protein: 1.4g, Fat: 7.4g*

## Fudge Popsicles

*Prep Time 10 minutes*

*Total Time 10 minutes*

*Servings 10*

*Ingredients*

1 teaspoon vanilla extract

3/4 cup almond milk, unsweetened

2 large eggs

1/3 cup stevia/erythritol blend, granulated

2 1/2 ounces baking chocolate finely chopped, unsweetened

1 3/4 cup grass-fed and organic heavy cream

*Directions*

1. Whisk together heavy cream, eggs, granulated sweetener and the baking chocolate in a 1 1/2 quart saucepan.

2. Put the saucepan that has the contents over medium low heat setting and continue to whisk without stopping until the ingredients come into a simmer.

3. Remove the mixture from heat and then whisk in vanilla extract and almond milk.

4. Add the mixture into popsicle molds, cover the popsicles and then insert the sticks.

5. Keep the popsicle sticks frozen for approximately 5 hours or so.

*Calories 207, Carbs 3g, Protein 3g, Fat 20g*

## Sugar-Free Fudge Pops

*Prep Time: 5 minutes*

*Cook Time: 5 minutes*

*Freezing Time 6 hours*

*Keto Ice Creams*

*Total Time: 6 hours 10 minutes*

*Servings: 8*

*Ingredients*

1/4 teaspoon xanthan gum

1 teaspoon peppermint extract or vanilla extract

1/3 cup unsweetened cocoa powder

1/3 cup Swerve Sweetener

1 cup unsweetened almond or cashew milk

1 cup heavy cream

*Directions*

1. Whisk cream, almond milk, cocoa powder and swerve over medium high heat inside a medium sauce pan.

2. Bring the contents to a boil and cook for approximately 1 minute, while stirring.

3. Then remove them the heat and add in peppermint extract. Distribute the xanthan gum evenly over the mixture and now whisk to mix.

4. Allow the mixture to cool down for approximately 10 minutes. you can then pour the cool mixture into the molds.

5. Keep the molds frozen for about 1 hour, and then push the popsicle sticks in the molds.

6. Transfer the molds into your freezer and keep everything frozen for another 5 hours, or until solid.

7. Finally run hot water over the molds for about 30 minutes to release the popsicles.

*Calories 118, Carbs 3.1g, Protein 1.44g, Fat 11.2g*

# Yogurt Pops

*Prep Time: 15 minutes*

*Total Time: 15 minutes*

*Serves 4*

*Ingredients*

8 – 10 drops liquid stevia

4 tablespoons lemon juice, divided

2 cups Greek yogurt, divided

1/2 cup blueberries, chopped

1/2 cup strawberries, chopped

*Directions*

1. Mix together half of the yogurt, strawberries, the sweetener and a tablespoon of lemon juice in a food processor or blender.

2. Puree until smooth and then move to a measuring cup or a bowl. Add in a tablespoon of lemon juice, ½ cup yogurt, preferred sweetener and blueberries.

3. Mix in the rest of the yogurt, sweetener and lemon juice and process until the contents have blended well.

4. Share the strawberry mixture among 8 paper cups or popsicle molds. Firmly tap the molds on the counter to make it well settle.

5. Share the yogurt mixture among cups or molds and tap firmly. Top the contents with the blueberry mixture and tap it well too.

6. At this point, put the molds in a freezer and keep frozen for about 1 hour. As soon as they begin to firm up, add in the popsicle sticks and freeze for another 2 to 3 hours, or until firm.

7. In case you want to go red, white and red, it's recommended to use 1 cup of strawberries and while omitting the blueberries.

8. Just process the strawberries with 2 tablespoons of lemon juice, a cup of yogurt and a sweetener of your choice.

9. Then layer the mixture on the bottom and at the top of your molds.

*Calories 99, Carbs 10.9g, Protein 4.6g, Fat 4.6g*

# Coconut Milk Popsicles

*Prep Time 5 minutes*

*Cook Time 5 minutes*

*Freezing time 2 hours*

*Total Time 10 minutes*

*Servings 6*

*Ingredients*

2 tablespoons mint leaves

1/2 ounce lime juice

1/2 cup blueberries

1 can coconut milk

*Directions*

1. In saucepan, heat some coconut milk along mint leaves for about 4 to 5 minutes.

2. Then remove the mixture from heat, and strain out the leaves. Set the coconut milk in a bowl to cool.

3. Mix together blueberries and lime juice for 4 to 5 minutes over low medium heat to make compote. Let the sugar-free compote to fully cool down.

4. As soon as the coconut milk is cool enough, fill 6 popsicle molds about 3/4 all the way.

5. In case you're using large molds, consider adding a little amount of water to each to boost the volume if required.

6. Transfer the molds in the freezer until almost set, or for 30 to 40 minutes.

7. You can then remove from the freezer and swirl in the sugar-free compote.

8. Add the sticks into the middle of the molds and keep everything frozen until the popsicles are fully frozen, or for about 2 hours.

*Calories 133, Carbs 3g, Protein 1g, Fat 13g*

# Raspberry Ice Cream Bars

*Serves 10 bars*

*Prep Time: 20 minutes*

*Additional Time: 4 hours*

*Total Time: 4 hours 20 minutes*

*Ingredients*

1 teaspoon vanilla

1/2 cup erythritol

4 cups of raspberries (2 cups juice)

2 cups of heavy cream

*Directions*

1. Begin by cooking the raspberries on low heat setting, along with a 1/2 cup of water until the juice in them release.

2. Then press the berries through a sieve and extract as much of the liquids as possible. Reserve 2 cups of this juice.

3. Add in a tablespoon of the low carb vodka. Combine powdered erythritol with vanilla and heavy cream and separate the mixture into two bowls.

4. Add in a tablespoon of vodka, and then add 1/2 cup of the reserved raspberry juice to one of heavy cream bowls, and the remaining 1 1/2 cups to the other bowl.

5. Move the mixture into a popsicle mod and alternate between individual colors. Pour the mixture carefully so as not to blend them.

6. Freeze the ice cream until solid and then remove from the mold.

7. Store the ice cream bars while wrapped with parchment paper in a freezer bag for not more than 1 month.

*Calories: 188 Fat: 17.9g Carbs: 7g Protein: 1.4g*

# Avocado Ice Cream Bars

*Prep Time 15 minutes*

*Passive time 2 hours*

*Total Time 2 hours 15 minutes*

*Servings 12*

*Ingredients*

2 tablespoons unsweetened coconut, shredded

1/4 cup Brazil nuts chopped

1/2 cup heavy cream

3 tablespoons Greek yogurt

10-20 drops liquid stevia

1 tablespoons lemon juice

2 avocados

*Directions*

1. Mix together everything apart from the nuts and the coconut in a high speed food processor or blender. Blend until you obtain a well incorporated mixture.

2. Move the mixture into a bowl and stir in the chopped nuts and shredded coconut. Add extra stevia if you like.

3. Cover the baking pan or baking sheet with parchment paper and spray some coconut oil over it.

4. Dust with additional shredded coconut and keep frozen for a minimum of 2 hours.

5. Remove the baking sheet from your freezer and cut the ice cream into square parts.

6. You can store the ice cream bars frozen for up to 1 month.

*Calories 117, Carbs 4g, Protein 2g, Fat 11g*

# Toasted Almond Ice Cream Bars

*Prep Time 10 minutes*

*Freeze time 6 minutes*

*Total Time 10 minutes*

*Servings: 9 bars*

*Ingredients*

1 1/2 cups ground almonds

2 teaspoons fresh lime juice

2 teaspoons pure almond extract

1/2 cup swerve, all natural sweetener

1 1/2 cups heavy cream

*Directions*

1. In a dry skillet, toast some almonds over medium heat for about 5 minutes while you stirring continuously to avoid burning. Set aside the skillet to cool down.

2. Whip some swerve and heavy cream in a large bowl until you obtain light and fluffy mixture.

3. Then stir fresh lime and almond extract and spoon a tablespoon of the toasted almonds into the bottom of a popsicle mold.

4. Fill the ice cream molds with the whipped mixture and then top with another layer of cooled toasted almonds.

5. Keep the ice cream molds frozen until solid, and then remove form the molds.

6. You can add sticks if you like. Serve!

*Calories 245, Carbs 10g, Protein 4g, Fat 23g*

# Homemade Snickers Ice Cream Bars

*Serves: 24 bars*

*Prep Time: 1 hour*

*Additional Time: 4 hours*

*Total Time: 5 hours*

*Ingredients*

2 tablespoons coconut oil

6.5 oz. 85% dark chocolate or unsweetened chocolate

1/2 cup peanuts

1 cup natural creamy peanut butter

1 1/2 cups heavy cream

4 oz. cream cheese

1/2 cup Keto caramel, (8 tablespoons heavy cream + 6 tablespoons butter)

*Directions*

1. Begin by making the caramel sauce using 8 tablespoons of heavy cream and 7 tablespoons of butter. Cool the caramel sauce and set it aside.

2. Beat cream cheese in a bowl using an electric heater and then gradually add in the heavy cream. You should scrap down the bowl to eliminate all lumps.

3. As soon as you've added all the heavy cream, beat the mixture until you obtain stiff peaks. Then fold in the peanut butter.

4. Now line a square pan measuring 9x9 inch with 2 parchment papers in a way that the parchment is hanging over each edge.

5. Lay the peanut butter mixture on the bottom of the parchment-lined pan and sprinkle uniformly with the peanuts. Press the peanuts lightly into the peanut butter mixture.

6. Drizzle the homemade caramel sauce over the peanuts and out the mixture into the freezer for a minimum of 3 hours, or if you like it overnight.

7. As soon as the ice cream is frozen, lift it from the pan using the parchment paper and place it on a cutting board.

8. Cut the bar into 24 equally sized bars and divide the bars into 2 sets. Put each 12 bars set on a baking sheet lined with parchment paper.

9. Return the ice cream bars to the freeze as you melt the chocolate. Just melt the chocolate in a double boiler along with some coconut oil, until melted.

10. You can also melt in the microwave for about 30 seconds and reheat at 10 seconds intervals while stirring in between until melted.

11. Dip each of the bar in the melted chocolate mixture using a fork, and tap of any excess. You should work with one sheet of bars at each dipping.

12. Return the ice cream bars into the baking sheet. As soon as all the ice creams are chocolate coated, return the baking sheet into your freezer and cover the second batch with chocolate too.

13. Then move all the chocolate covered ice cream bars to an airtight container and keep frozen for not more than 3 months.

*Calories: 216 Fat: 20.3g Carbs: 3.4g Protein: 5g*

# Yogurt Berry Ice Blocks

*Prep Time 5 minutes*

*Total Time 5 minutes*

*Serves 6*

*Ingredients*

2 tablespoons granulated sweetener

150 ml coconut cream

150 ml natural yogurt, unsweetened

125g fresh or frozen berries

*Directions*

1. In a measuring jug, mash the granulated sweetener and the berries with a fork.

2. Then add yogurt and coconut cream and combine well.

3. Transfer the mixture into ice cube trays or ice blocks.

4. Keep it frozen preferably overnight.

*Calories 86, Carbs 3.5g, Protein 2.3g, Fat 6.5g*

*Keto Ice Creams*

# Peanut Butter Ice Cream Bars

*Prep Time 10 minutes*

*Freezing Time 3 hours*

*Total Time 3 hours 10 minutes*

*Servings 10 bars*

*Ingredients*

1/4 cup erythritol

1/2 cup salted peanut butter, unsweetened

1 teaspoon vanilla extract

1/2 cup+2 tablespoons almond milk, unsweetened

3/4 cup heavy cream

*For the Chocolate Magic Shell*

1/3 cup coconut oil

2/3 cup chocolate chips, sugar free

*Directions*

1. First, whip the heavy cream using a mixer until you obtain soft peaks.

2. Then gradually add in the rest of the ingredients.

3. Beat the mixture until you obtain soft peaks and then pour it into molds.

4. Add in the popsicle sticks and keep the ice cream frozen for more than 3 hours.

5. At this point, melt the Magic Shell ingredients and then remove the ice cream from the freezer.

6. Dip the ice cream into the coconut oil and chocolate mixture and allow to set.

7. Keep the ice cream bars in airtight and move them to your freezer until ready to serve.

*Calories 170, Carbs 4.5g, Protein 3.4g, Fat 8.7g*

# Low-Carb Ice Cream Bars

*Prep Time: 35 minutes*

*Cook Time: 10 minutes*

*Chill Time 1-2 hours*

*Total Time: 1 hour 45 minutes*

*Servings: 12*

*Ingredients*

30g cacao nibs

100g raspberries fresh or frozen

2 teaspoons vanilla

4 tablespoons granulated sweetener

750 ml coconut cream

8 egg yolks

*Directions*

1. In a saucepan, add in egg yolks and the coconut cream and place on a stove.

2. Then heat the ingredients under low heat for about 10 minutes or until the coconut cream starts to thicken.

3. Take out from the heat and then add in vanilla and erythritol. Adjust the flavor depending on your liking.

4. Let the contents cool down and then stir in cacao nibs and raspberries.

5. Transfer the mixture into a metal baking dish line with plastic wrap or a just a silicon dish.

6. Put the mixture in your freezer until well frozen.

7. You can then remove and cut it into 12 ice cream bars.

*Calories 248, Carbs 4.6g, Protein 4.6g, Fat 23.5g*

# Keto Ice Cream Bars

*Prep time: 5 minutes*

*Total time: 5 minutes*

*Serves: 4*

*Ingredients*

1 teaspoon strawberry or raspberry extract

¼ cup Swerve confectioners'

1 cup almond milk, unsweetened

1 cup heavy cream or coconut milk

*Directions*

1. Process everything in a blender until fully combined. Then pour the contents in to your popsicle molds.

2. Move the molds into the freezer and keep them chilled for a minimum of 2 hours and then serve.

3. Store the ice cream bars covered until ready to serve, but you should eat them within 1 month.

*Calories 114, Carbs 1.3g, Protein 0.9g, Fat 12g*

# Mocha Ice Cream Bars

*Prep Time: 15 minutes*

*Cook Time: 15 minutes*

*Cool Time: 4 hours*

*Total Time: 4 hours 30 minutes*

*Serves 8-12*

*Ingredients*

2 ounces sugar-free chocolate

1/2 teaspoon vanilla extract

3 egg yolks

1 teaspoon instant espresso powder

1/2 cup Swerve Sweetener

2 teaspoons grass-fed gelatin

3 cups full fat coconut milk, divided

*Directions*

1. Add half cup of coconut milk along with some gelatin in a medium saucepan. Allow to stand for a few minutes then set

the heat to medium. Whisk the mixture until gelatin has dissolved.

2. Add in the rest of coconut milk, instant coffee and the sweetener and stir the mixture until the coffee and the sweetener dissolve. The temperature on the instant read thermometer should be at approximately 175 degree F.

3. Now in a medium sized bowl, whisk the 3 egg yolks for a few seconds. Add in a cup of the hot coffee and coconut milk mixture and continue to whisk to temper the yolks.

4. Whisk this egg yolk mixture back into cream as you continue to whisk constantly.

5. At this point, cook the mixture until it reaches 180 degrees F on the instant read thermometer.

6. Remove the mixture from heat and pour it over an ice bath; let cool until no longer hot to touch, or for up to 15 minutes.

7. Stir in the vanilla extract and share the mixture among 12 small Popsicle molds. Keep it frozen for around 40 minutes before inserting a wooden stick around 2/3 into each of them.

8. Then freeze the contents for 3 hours or so. Meanwhile, melt the chocolate in a bowl that is placed on simmering water.

9. Once done, unmold the Popsicles from the molds by running hot water over them for 20 to 30 seconds.

10. Set them on a prepared or waxed paper-lined baking sheet, and then return them into the freezer.

11. Hold each of the Popsicle over the bowl one at a time and drizzle with the chocolate, and turn to get all sides.

12. Keep it the freezer and repeat the process with the rest of the popsicles.

*Calories 235, Carbs 6g, Protein 3.8g, Fat 21.65g*

# Iced Coffee and Tea Frozen Treats

## Coffee Panna Cotta with Raspberry

*Prep Time: 45 minutes*

*Cook Time: 10 minutes*

*Total Time: 55 minutes*

*Serves 8*

*Ingredients*

*Coffee Panna Cotta:*

10 drops stevia extract

1/2 teaspoon vanilla extract

1 1/2 cups Greek yogurt

1/3 cup Swerve Sweetener

1 tablespoons instant coffee

1 envelope gelatin, unflavored

1 1/2 cups heavy cream divided

*Raspberry Coulis:*

2 teaspoons fresh lemon juice

3 tablespoons Swerve Sweetener, powdered

2 cups fresh or frozen raspberries, raw

*Directions*

1. To make the panna cotta, slightly grease 8 serving dishes or 8 half-cup ramekins.

2. Put the half cup heavy cream in a saucepan along with some gelatin and let the mixture sit for approximately 3 minutes.

3. Add in the rest of the cream, granulated erythritol and the instant coffee and set the mixture over medium heat.

4. Whisk until the granulated erythritol, coffee and gelatin are entirely dissolved. Cook until the contents start to steam, but don't boil.

5. Remove the mixture from heat and now stir in stevia, vanilla and the yogurt. Heat while stirring until smooth.

6. Share the mixture the mixture among the well-greased ramekins, and wrap in plastic wrap. Keep everything for a minimum 3 hours.

7. To make the raspberry coulis, blend the powdered erythritol and raspberries in a food processor until smooth.

8. Set a fine mesh over a medium-sized bowl and now drain, while pressing on the solids so as to obtain highest possible amount of liquids.

9. Then stir in some lemon juice.

10. To unmold the panna cotta, just place the ramekin in a couple of inches of hot water and then run a knife around the outside and invent it on a prepared plate.

11. You can also let the panna cotta remain in the serving dish and now drizzle with the raspberry coulis. Serve and enjoy.

*Calories 104, Carb 14.8g, Protein 2.2g, Fat 4.0g*

## Mocha Ice Cream

*Prep Time: 35 minutes*

*Cook Time: 10 minutes*

*Chill Time 4 hours*

*Total Time: 4 hours 45 minutes*

*Serves 2*

*Ingredients*

¼ teaspoon xanthan gum

1 tablespoon instant coffee

2 tablespoons cocoa powder, unsweetened

15 drops liquid Stevia

2 tablespoons erythritol

¼ cup heavy whipping cream

1 cup coconut milk

*Directions*

1. Add everything to a bowl that can comfortably hold an immersion blender, apart from xanthan gum.

2. Using an immersion blender, puree the ingredients until well incorporated.

3. Then gently add in the sweetener until the mixture begins to thicken. Add extra amounts of the xanthan gum if you like it.

4. Now add everything to your ice cream maker and churn according to the manufacturer's directions.

5. Serve immediately! You can add in instant coffee if you like or garnish with some mint.

*Calories 175, Carbs 10.36g, Protein 2.59g, Fats 14.98g*

## Coffee Ice Cream

*Prep Time 25 minutes*

*Cook Time 40 minutes*

*Total Time 1 hour 5 minutes*

*Servings 7*

*Ingredients*

1/8 teaspoon kosher salt

1/2 teaspoon vanilla extract

1 teaspoon coffee extract or instant powder

1 teaspoon xanthan gum

1 1/2 tablespoons Vanilla Honest Syrup

1/2 teaspoon stevia concentrated powder

1/4 cup inulin or allulose white sweetener

2 cups heavy cream

1 cup unsweetened almond or coconut milk

1/4 cup strong brewed coffee

1 1/2 ounces or 3 tablespoons cream cheese softened

Ice water

*Directions*

1. Add ice water to a large bowl until full, then whisk cream cheese in a separate bowl until smooth.

2. Mix together heavy cream, almond milk, brewed coffee, stevia extract powder, and the VitaFiber syrup and fiber.

3. Bring the mixture to a gentle boil and cook on medium heat settings for approximately 4 minutes.

4. Then stir in vanilla, coffee powder or extract and the xanthan gum.

5. Carefully whisk in the hot almond milk mixture into the whisked cream cheese until well blended. Whisk in some salt.

6. Set the bowl with the mixture in ice water bath and allow to stand for around 20 minutes or until cold while stirring now and again.

7. Move the mixture into an ice cream machine and freeze it as per the ice cream maker's directions.

8. Move the ice cream into a plastic container and wrap with a plastic sheet.

9. Close the container with an airtight lid and keep the ice cream frozen for approximately 4 hours, or until set.

*Calories: 265, Carbs: 12.6g, Protein: 1.7g, Fat: 24g*

# Keto Coffee Ice Cream

*Prep Time: 15 minutes*

*Total Time: 15 minutes*

*Serves: 2*

*Ingredients:*

1-2 teaspoons pure vanilla extract

2-4 tablespoons Monkfruit sweetener

1 double shot of Bulletproof Espresso Coffee

13 ounces of coconut cream that have been frozen into ice cubes

2 ripe avocados, roughly diced and frozen

Whole coffee beans, optional

1 tablespoon water or Brain Octane Oil or water, optional

*Directions*

1. Remove the frozen avocados and the coconut cubes from your freezer and then let them thaw for about 5 to 10 minutes.

2. Add everything beginning with the Monkfruit sweetener to a food processor or blender and process until you get creamy and smooth ice cream.

3. Keep scrapping down the edges of your blender and then process a couple of times.

4. In case you find it hard to blend until smooth, add in a tablespoon of water or Brain Octane Oil gradually until you achieve the creamy consistency.

5. Taste the ice cream and adjust the flavor if required. Then scoop the ice cream into 2 bowls and then enjoy.

*Calories: 596. Carbs: 20.5g. Protein: 6.3g, Fat: 61g*

# Dairy-Free Coffee Ice Cream

*Prep Time: 30 minutes*

*Cooling/Freezing Time: 8 hours*

*Total Time: 8 hours 30 minutes*

*Serves: 8*

*Ingredients*

¼ teaspoons stevia extract

1 teaspoons organic vanilla extract

2 tablespoons raw coconut nectar

1 cup organic coffee, double strength

0.125 teaspoons sea salt

2 teaspoons gelatin, unflavored

48 tablespoons organic coconut milk

1 oz. Kahlua

*Directions*

1. To a medium saucepan, add the organic coffee and then simmer to reduce the amount to ½ cup.

2. Using gelatin, sprinkle the organic coffee well and then warm it over low heat, until the gelatin fully dissolves. You don't need to stir.

3. Now in a blender, spoon all of your coffee mixture and then blend until it's smooth. Add the coconut nectar, stevia and sea salt and continue to blend.

4. Then add in vanilla, milk and Kahlua and continue to blend. Once done, pour into your glass container and cool for 6 hours while covered to constitute a custard-like substance.

5. Transfer into a freezer bowl of your ice cream maker and continue to make the ice cream based on the directions of the appliance maker.

6. Freeze for about 2 hours until it turn firm.

*Calories 178, Carbs 10.9g, Protein 3.7g, Fat 15g*

# Green Tea Ice Cream

*Prep Time 40 minutes*

*Total Time 40 minutes*

*Servings 5*

*Ingredients*

1 1/2 cup heavy cream

1/2 cup almond milk, unsweetened

1/2 cup Swerve

4 green tea bags

1/3 cup boiling water

*Directions*

1. Begin by putting the tea bags into the boiling water inside a cup.

2. Then allow to steep as required, for about 5 minutes or so.

3. Once done, start brewing the tea in the boiling water. Simply squeeze the tea from individual teabags and then discard them.

4. Then add in a sweetener of choice such as swerve to the hot tea. Set it aside until cool enough to handle.

5. At this point, stir in the unsweetened almond milk along with the heavy cream.

6. Then pour the mixture into the canister of an ice cream maker and churn according to the manufacturer's directions.

7. Serve the ice cream instantly for best flavor and store any remainder in the freezer. To serve the frozen ice cream, you should thaw it for a few minutes before serving.

8. If you don't have a churning machine, you can whip the mixture using an electric beater until it has thickened and then store in the freezer.

9. Keep stirring the mixture at intervals of about 20 minutes up until you obtain the consistency of an ice cream that you like.

*Calories 249, Carbs 2.1g, Protein 1.5g, Fat 25.6g*

## Conclusion

Thank you for purchasing this book.

With those amazingly delicious ice creams and frozen treats, you are sure to enjoy your ketogenic journey.

All the best in your quest for a healthier YOU.

Finally, I would like to ask you for a favor. Can you please leave a review for this book? I will greatly appreciate that.

Thank you and Good Luck!

# About The Author

For most of my life, I did not have to worry too much about my weight; I was not the fittest person but I was also not overweight, which was good enough for me. However, after I gave birth to my lovely son, things changed; I gained quite a bit of weight and I did not like what I saw. I was not as confident as I once was and I was very conscious of how I looked and how the clothes I wore made me look. Once my son turned one and was not breastfeeding as much, I started researching for ways to lose weight.

In my quest to lose weight, I have tried quite a bit of different things from the ketogenic diet and intermittent fasting to smoothie cleanses. Since all these have worked for me, I have incorporated them into my lifestyle and I must say, so far I like what I see.

I understand how difficult losing weight can be and to make it easier for you, I write books on what has worked for me and how you can lose weight to achieve your desired body.

I have still not achieved my dream body but I am happy with the progress so far and that is good enough because life is not perfect and I am okay with good enough.

# My Other Books

If you love this book, I have other ketogenic diet books that may interest you.

## Keto Bread

https://www.amazon.com/Keto-Bread-Flatbread-Tortillas-Cornbread-ebook/dp/B07S16MNGM/ref=sr_1_64?keywords=Keto+bread&qid=1565622803&s=digital-text&sr=1-64

## Keto Fat Bombs

https://www.amazon.com/Keto-Fat-Bombs-Optimal-Ketosis-ebook/dp/B07RVPKGL7/ref=sr_1_1?keywords=Keto+fat+bombs%3A+over+70+sweet+and+savory&qid=1565623307&s=digital-text&sr=1-1

## Keto Meal Plan

https://www.amazon.com/Keto-Meal-Plan-Ketogenic-Deliciousebook/dp/B07R4JSC2B/ref=sr_1_1?keywords=keto+meal+plan%3A+90+day+ketogenic&qid=1565623382&s=digital-text&sr=1-1

## The Simple 5 Ingredient Keto Cookbook

https://www.amazon.com/Simple-Ingredient-Keto-Cookbook-Ingredients-ebook/dp/B07R6BH3JK/ref=sr_1_8?keywords=the+simple+5+ingredient+keto+cookbook&qid=1565623477&s=digital-text&sr=1-8

## Keto Air fryer Recipes

https://www.amazon.com/dp/B07WFQTXQN

Made in United States
Troutdale, OR
12/20/2024